List Building Strategies That Work

Start Building A Buyers List From Scratch

By Liudas Butkus

Table of Contents

Hi,

Thank you for purchasing this book, where I'm going to teach you how to build a buyers list.

Most of the books and courses out there only talk how to build a regular email list. Sure, building a list is important, but they forget to mention that there are actually two main types of lists that you can build:

1. A list of freebie seekers

2. A list of buyers

In this book we will focus on building that buyers list aka customers list. You have most definitely heard the saying: money is in the list, which is true, but more accurate to say is that the money is in the buyers list.

So, instead of teaching you how to build a regular list like everyone else is building I will teach you how to build a list of buyers regardless of whether they bought from you directly or from your "competitors". The strategies that I'm going to share with you will build your buyers list fast.

Also, as a bonus for buying this book I want to give you a free training on Facebook advertising. Click here!

Regardless of what kind of online business you are running or even an offline businesses, you need to have a strong following of customers – people who are willing to spend money and buy from you. So it's necessary to build a buyers list, if you want to have a successful business.

Now, what are the advantages of building a buyers list over a freebie seeker list? Well, there are 2 main benefits:

1. A buyers list is more responsive than a Freebie seekers list, though I'm not saying not to build a regular list ever. It's still important to have a freebie seekers list because they can potentially buy from you and get to your buyers list, but you will firstly need to build rapport with them to gain trust for that sale to happen.

So, you should be building both of these lists, but keep in mind that your goal is to convert as much of those freebie seekers into buyers.

2. If a person is on a buyers list it means that sometime in the past he has used his credit card to buy something online and that makes him more responsive. Converting a freebie

seeker into a buyer takes a lot of time and effort. It can take months of building rapport with them until they are ready to buy, whereas a buyer is already familiar with you, you have built rapport with him so, he has trust in your products and that makes selling for you so much easier.

Also, people who have bought something online are more likely to do it again. A buyer is a buyer is a buyer.

A buyer list will always be smaller than a general list, but you should keep in mind that a subscriber from a buyers list on average will generate you ten times more revenue than a general freebie seeker.

So, in general buyers are top level subscribers. They have already bought something and chances are they are going to buy again.

Building a customers list can be challenging because usually, you need to build a prospects list FIRST before you can try to convert into customers. At least that's what the majority of list building courses teach you.

Wouldn't it be cool, if you could skip building the freebie seekers list and start with building a buyers list instead? Hell yeah and it actually is possible, you can start building your buyers list even, if you currently have zero subscribers on your list.

In this book I reveal 5 powerful strategies for building a buyers list:

- The Membership Pass Strategy
- The Instant 100% Commissions Plan
- Launch Bonus Jacking Method
- Viral Resell Rights Method
- Bonus Webinar Method

You don't need to use all of these methods. Choose the one that you like most implement and you will get results, any of these strategies have the potential of building you a huge buyers list. So, don't overwhelm yourself. Pick one, learn it, implement it and then add another and another until you are using them all or maybe you will decide to only use two or three of them.

I'm explaining these methods with the assumption that you don't have a list yet and that you don't have a huge starting budget.

In case you are wondering, it doesn't matter that much, if these people haven't bought from you directly or not. As long as they have bought something from someone they are still higher quality leads.

So the premise of this book is to teach you how to build yourself a list of paid customers; people who have previously bought something from anyone and you want to get them to join your mailing list. Remember to keep this list extra special and at the end of this course, I will teach you what to do with the buyers list and how to maximize your profits and benefits as well.

Membership Pass Strategy

For the membership pass strategy to work you will need to create a high quality membership site, which can be sold. We won't be building a free membership site.

To join this membership site people will have to pay money first, if they want to get access.

You will also need to have an upsell and you will be giving away commissions for that upsell to your affiliates, this will help you get people to promote you membership site.

Once you have your membership site ready with an upsell offer, you're going to contact other membership site owners or mailing list owners to give this membership pass away as a bonus. DO NOT label it as 'FREE' even though it is. It should be positioned as a bonus. Make it a special bonus membership ONLY for their customers.

As you can imagine, you're going to come up with a paid membership site but you are going to give it away as a bonus to other people's customers. This is going to help add value to their customers and the webmaster will also earn a commission from the upsell.

REPEAT THIS with as many membership site owners and mailing list owners as you can and you will get yourself a list of paid buyers in no time.

Here's how the membership plan goes:

Offer lifetime access. DO NOT offer any trial or monthly access in this case! Speaking from experience, usually people have a tendency to just join a trial and then cancel before they get billed. And even for those people who continue to carry on, they will probably cancel a few months later. This is not a good way to handle your new list of potential customers because once they leave your membership site, they will most likely not going to return. So the best thing to do is to offer lifetime access with no strings attached.

No forced regular updates required. This is good for you as well because there won't be forced regular updates on your part. You don't have to keep updating and adding content to your membership site every month.

Though this book isn't focused on creating a membership site, here are some ideas for it:

Format: articles, audio, videos, hosted software

You can put all these in the members' area. As for hosting software, you can go for web based software in which requires people to log in to your membership site in order to use your software. This is something a lot of Internet marketers are doing right now.

The same goes with videos and audio, you can create value by allowing members to only view their videos in the membership site rather than they download and not log in again.

Theme: browse popular marketplaces like ClickBank and see what's trending.

You can quickly do research on ClickBank and see what's currently hot and selling. If there are several products with high gravity in a niche then it's a viable niche to make money. If you already have a niche that you are working in and it's a popular niche than you can definitely skip this.

Now how do you get content for your membership site WITHOUT creating it yourself?

Here are 5 easy ways to get valuable content without creating it yourself:

1. Curate content from other sites. You can find related content by doing a Google search pretty much on any topic. When you find an article you like copy and paste it in your members area and make sure you have a link back to the original article. Some sites like about.com or many news sites don't allow you to do that so, I would avoid them, but there's still plenty of blogs and other sites that you can use. There are membership sites doing pretty well with this method.

2. Public Domain. Public domain content is basically old content dated from hundred years; content created before 1st January 1923.Content in public domain can include books, articles, reports, film and so on. Since the copyrights have long expired, it means that they are usually copy right-free and you can take their works.

Obviously you won't find tons of public domain content in every niche, but there are some great evergreen content, mostly in the self-improvement niche that you could use.

3. Private Label Rights. What private label rights mean is that you can take a product, edit the content as you like, change the name, add your own insights and then sell it as your own keeping all of the profits.

There are tons of PLR content in all the big niches out there. Though finding free PLR content that is high quality might be challenging, but it isn't impossible. A few good sites where you can find both free and paid PLR content are: http://resell-rights-weekly.com/ and http://master-resell-rights.com.lk/

If you happen to find PLR videos make sure to use them because video is super powerful these days.

4. YouTube Videos. Speaking of videos, you can also get some really good videos from YouTube. You can embed or share links to relevant videos and put them on your site. It may be free but it is quality content and you save your customers the time on searching on their own.

5. Author Contributions/Interviews. If you have connections with authors or experts, you

can choose to interview or ask them to contribute something to your membership site. It can be a short article or even a report. In return, you are helping the authors and experts spreading their work. So you get content for your membership site and they in return get exposure -- certainly a win-win situation.

Now, the reason you want to build a membership site instead of a regular downloadable product is that people will need to go to the membership site multiple times to access all the content and that helps you build rapport with them, which will help you get more sales in the future.

Don't worry, if you have no idea how to create a membership site, with today's technologies it's cheap, easy and fast to create one.

Here are 2 different ways that you can use to create a membership site:

1. aMember Pro. If you don't mind spending a little bit of money, I suggest you to invest in aMember. It is an excellent software that manages your membership site and you can have multiple membership levels. The

installation is usually free when you purchase a copy of your aMember. Get it installed and you are good to go.

2. Wordpress + Plugin. Alternatively, you can install Wordpress and then use one out of many membership site plugins. Some plugins that you can choose from: MemberWing, WPMembers and there's many more that you can find.

Now, we will talk how to build your upsell offer.

The entry level to join the membership is going to be free, but you ned to position this that it's free only to the customers of your partner and to make them feel that they are getting a great deal, which they are, if you created a good product.

Once they join you will want to upsell immediately - When a person joins your membership site, you must present an upsell immediately (also known as a one-time offer). Price it anywhere from $37 - $77.

Have a down sell at half price to get more sales. If they don't buy the upsell you don't want to give up yet. You want to offer them a downsel. Don't worry it doesn't need to be yet another product, just remove some of the content from the original package and have it at a lower price. So, if people don't buy your upsell you will have a second chance of making money from them with your downsell.

Give 75% - 100% commissions to your promotion partner - Since your membership site should have an affiliate program, you are going to give anywhere from 75% to 100% commission to your promotion partner. Why you are willing to give away so much is because this will encourage them to give away your membership pass for free because for every upgrade, they are going to get a commission. The more valuable you can make the opportunity to your partner the better because if they don't accept your proposal you won't build a list.

So once you have that membership site in place, here's how to contact other membership owners and important points to include in your proposal.

When you write them an e-mail or find them through Skype or any other means of communication, mention that you have a paid membership site that is currently selling in the market place BUT only for his customers or paid members, they can get access to your membership site free, as a valuable bonus.

When the membership owners give this access away to their customers whether through their own members area or mailing list, they will join and see an upgrade or a one-time offer. For every one of them who purchases, the partner will get credited commissions. So you can leave this bonus in the membership area and collect passive income. You can propose this to the membership site owner.

It is surprisingly easy to find product owners in any given niche that has rabid trends. When you find out their websites, you can drop them an e-mail or contact them via their forms.

Do a Google search for the name of the niche you are in and put in the keyword "membership" so that you'll get results full of mainstream membership sites for your selected niche.

Once you find out what these membership sites are, you can join them for free or pay for your access to them. Normally you can find other authors and experts related to the membership site

since they are all related to the same niche. So this will help you find more referrals as well.

The Instant 100% Commissions

You know what's the fastest way to build a customer list? Offer 100% instant commissions! There are four good reasons why you should do this:

1. People love getting paid instantly vs. waiting for 30 days or more -If you are an affiliate marketer, you know how frustrating it is to wait to get paid for the sales you have already done.

2. Healthy Cash Flow for Everyone - If you pay your affiliates instantly they will be more motivated to continue promoting you. Also, they will have an instant cash flow, which they can use to buy more advertising.

3. Refunds - As far as refunds are concerned, your affiliates can handle it on their own because the payment will go to them and for any reason at all the customer wants to ask for a refund, they are able to refund the money back to the customers.

4. No worries about paying manually every month –You don't have to worry about paying manually every month anymore. The moment you pay your affiliates immediately, the

responsibility gets off your back and you can focus on other matters rather than to do last minute calculations.

There are several sites that you can use to set-up offers and payout 100% commissions to your affiliates.

- WarriorPlus
- JVZoo

There are definitely more sites out there, but these are the ones that I highly recommend using.

These sites will handle all your payments for you and they also work as marketplaces. Once you set-up your product there you get instantly visible to all the affiliates on the platform.

I enjoy JVZoo a lot because you can set-up a product without any upfront costs. They will take a small fee from every payment that you get.

Next, you're going to learn how to start an instant commission strategy step-by-step.

It can be an E-book or a special report – it doesn't have to be something jam packed; just something that one can buy and consume quickly then be done with it. You can price it anywhere from $7 - $37.

Get affiliates promoting and set your commissions to preferably 100%. Try not to set for anything less than that as 100% commissions is the most ideal. This means that people who are promoting you will get paid straight into their PayPal account.

As for pricing your products, if you choose to price your products at anywhere from $7 to $17, I recommend you have a one-time offer priced at $37 to $47 so that you can maximize your affiliates' profits here. With that, your affiliates will be more inclined to promote you because they trust they can earn more bucks from you.

If however your frontend product is already priced at $37 and above, then it is not really necessary to have a one-time offer.

Do remember to credit your affiliates about 50% to 100% commissions on the one-time offer sales. When you motivate a group of affiliates to promote for you, you will be able to build your buyers list a lot quicker. Even though the money may not go to you directly at first, you can always make up in the backend sales where the real profits are. This will be discussed further at the end of this book.

As for finding affiliates to help you promote, there are 3 places to look at.

1. The Warrior Forum JV section. For first timers, one of the easiest places you can find affiliates to promote would be the WarriorForum. Look up at the joint venture section where people make joint venture offers. You can contact them via private message or reply in their threads. Alternatively, you can also put in your offers and try to group your own joint venture partners in the forum.

2. JVZoo and WarriorPlus have their own market place as mentioned earlier whereby once you have a product listed in their market place, you can count on getting affiliates promoting for you especially if your product is really good.

3. Join marketing groups on Facebook or other social media sites, build connections with other people in your marketplace, try to help them out first and only then ask for a favor to promote your offer.

Stick to your end goal regardless, you shouldn't mind your affiliates getting all the money because ultimately you want to get their leads into your customers list.

Some people don't really like this concept of giving away 100% commissions for all the hard work they put in creating the product, but if you really want to succeed you need to sacrifice your short term gains for long term profits. Once you have built that buyers list you will make so much more money. Still, remember that you are giving away 50% on the upsells so, you are still making money.

Launch Bonus Jacking

So far in my observation, Launch Bonus Jacking method has not really been used often however the few marketers who are using it are getting great results. Like the first method I've discussed, you have a valuable offer that you can actually sell or is currently selling so when promoting other people's product as an affiliate partner, you can ask to put this bonus offer in his Thank You Page.

This works brilliantly if you are promoting other people's product launches because it is the prime time of getting lots of customers. Moreover, this adds value and appeals to a customer especially if this is positioned as an unannounced bonus.

But the question now is how to come up with some offers and what kind?

There is no limit or rules imposed on what your offer should be, however bear in mind that a bonus functions as a complementary to the main product. It can be in the form of a membership pass, which was discussed extensively in Method #1 earlier.

You can also come up with your own video tutorials, or an exceptional special report detailing case studies or research material.

Regardless of what your offers are, you have to put up your opt-in form and require people to sign up to get your bonus. Remind them that this is a special bonus and not some free stuff that is available elsewhere.

If you can drive in substantial sales and promotion, for your partner then you are more likely to get your proposal approved. Make sure the offer is relevant to the product launch so that his customers may benefit from it.

For example if the product is about dating, then you have to make sure your product is complementary to that. Maybe creating something like "how to set-up your online dating profile".

Findng new launches in your niche can be a little bit challenging. So, you should actively participate in the community and look out for new launches. However, if you are looking to build a list in the internet marketing niche then you can find new launches easily on sites like: WarriorJV and MunchEye. It's easy to find contact information there as well.

Viral Resell Rights

First and foremost if you are not familiar with resell rights and master resell rights, here are the basic explanations:

Basic Resell Rights allows your customers to resell the products however, their customers cannot resell them. So this means that only your customers have the rights to resell your products.

Master Resell Rights on the other hand allows your customers to not only sell your product, but their customers can also resell the products and in turn so on and on.

In this case, I am going to teach you how to use Master Resell Rights to build your mailing list on warp speed and we're talking about a paid buyers list here.

The first step is to offer a Master Resell Rights to an E-book. You want to use an E-book because it's easier to rebrand and download than video or audio. It will also be easier for you to create it.

Include a sales kit to make it as easy as possible for your customers to resell it. A sales kit usually includes images of the product, resell right licenses and a sales letter. They are allowed to pass on the reselling opportunity to their own customers as well.

Check out how the reseller's kit should look like by downloading several PLR or MRR products from the websites listed in the first strategy.

IMPORTANT! Never offer your report with giveaway rights! A product being sold is more valuable and has a more viral effect than an E-book with giveaway rights. Ironically, there is no real motivation in giving away a product whereas there is more energy and enthusiasm in selling a product.

So when all has been done, what happens next? Imagine the following scenario:

You can sell the Master Resell Rights opportunity to your customers. Then your customers will sell it and their customers will also sell it and so will their customers in turn do the same! Bear in mind that all these are paid customers except that your own resellers are earning the money – not you directly.

In the E-book, include an incentive for people to visit your website and join your mailing list.

It should be something complimentary and something that doesn't stand out too much because, if it's a blatant promotion people will not want to resell it.

So how exactly do you create a Master Resell Rights product? The first step is to create a few E-books of 30 – 40 pages each. The next step is to create a reseller kit for each of the E-books. It must include a sales letter and a Thank You Page.

The most important part to make this strategy work is to have a link back to your website to generate those leads. If you don't have a link in the E-book then you won't be building a list.

Next step is to blast the Master Resell Rights offer to your mailing list (if you already have a list of your own) but make sure it is priced rather low i.e. $17 to $37.

This is because you want to make the product as sellable as possible. Pricing the product too high will make it harder for your customers to resell it and since most countries are not bound by their price fixing law, people generally resell their product for a lower price therefore you should start with a low price.

Alternatively, you submit them to Resell Rights membership sites.

Bonus Webinar Method

This is yet another rare method that is hardly used. Despite that it may be underutilized but it is highly effective. You might want to apply this method as soon as possible before the trend catches on.

Conducting a webinar for other people's customers; you offer to conduct a 1 to 2 hours webinar presentation for the latest product launches as a bonus. So you make sure you have a backend offer to pitch at the end of the call and it must be a high ticket product. Split 40 to 60% commissions with your partner.

www.GoToWebinar.com is an excellent webinar software tool with various plans. It is something that a lot of marketers are using. This is really an awesome webinar software tool that allows you to broadcast your presentation to hundreds of people.

Now, a free alternative to this would be doing a Google Hangout. There's no limitation to how many people can attend the class and it's completely free.

The offer at the end of the webinar has to be a high ticket one. Starting from $97 to $497 or more. It can be anything along the lines of 'done for you' products, home study courses or even a group or one-on-one coaching.

It has to be a high end exclusive offer because you are expecting to take fewer more exclusive customers.

The best part is that even if you only sell a few of your products, you will be building a list, which is much bigger than that, because you will be building a list of people who registered for the webinar and all of these people are buyers that your partner sent.

Here are additional places where you can look for those high scale launches, because small launches won't work well for this strategy.

- IMNewsWatch.com – news on latest marketing products launches
- JVNotify.com – you get advanced notifications on upcoming launches which give you head start to contact these potential launch partners
- Subscribe to mailing lists of a few experts who are on top of the niche.
- You can also use Google Alerts to receive notifications whenever Google picks up a

new website which contains some of your important keywords.

Summary

You now have all these methods to build your buyers list, but what will you do once you have built one?

Have backend products that you promote through your autoresponder. Start out with a mid ticket product of $27 - $57. You don't want it to be too expensive because it can be hard to get sales. This might be the first chance for you to finally make money depending on the methods you are going to be using so, you want to have yourself positioned to make as much sales as possible.

You can also create a membership site to generate recurring revenue, much like the site we talked in the first method.

Affiliate products are also a good idea to generate revenue. You can find them on sites that I have mentioned before ClickBank, JVZoo, WarriorPlus and many more.

For the main product your try to promote make sure that you have several follow-up emails to get higher conversions because usually people won't buy from the first email you send.

And some warnings on what to do and what NOT to do with your buyers list:

- DO NOT spoil them with too many free gifts! If you start giving too many freebies and spoil them with bonuses, they will be less inclined to buy anything from you later on. This in result will make them expect free things from you.
- Treat your Buyers List with extra special care. For example if you are selling your own product, it is best to give them special treatment. It could be in a form of a discount or extra bonuses but never overload them with freebies as mentioned above.
- Additionally, do not make them look as if they are getting the same deals as those from the general subscribers list otherwise they will not see the distinction and they might just leave your buyers list. Give them privileges and they will want to stay in your buyers list.
- Remember to keep in touch with them frequently. If you intend to keep in touch with them at least once a week, that

should be the way. It is best not to do it on an irregular basis like contacting them 5 times a week and then in the next week, you don't talk to them at all. Try to keep your communications consistent.

I hope you learned a lot from this book, but just knowing how to build a buyers list isn't enough, you need to put these strategies into action. Take the time to work on them every single day and you will start seeing results.

Sincerely,

Liudas Butkus

EasyM6.com

www.ingramcontent.com/pod-product-compliance
Lightning Source LLC
Chambersburg PA
CBHW070745180526
45168CB00004B/1543